W9-ANB-112

CREATING
PARTY FAVORS

Written by Dana Meachen Rau and Illustrated by Kathleen Petelinsek

CHERRY LAKE PUBLISHING • ANN ARBOR, MICHIGAN

Published in the United States of America by Cherry Lake Publishing
Ann Arbor, Michigan
www.cherrylakepublishing.com

Photo Credits: Page 4, ©gosphotodesign/Shutterstock; page 5,
©mary981/Shutterstock; page 6, ©paulaphoto/Shutterstock; page 7,
©Sergey Novikov/Shutterstock ; page 29, ©auremar/Shutterstock

Library of Congress Cataloging-in-Publication Data
Rau, Dana Meachen, 1971– author.
  Creating party favors / by Dana Meachen Rau.
     pages cm. — (How-to library)
  Summary: "Follow along with these fun projects to create party favors
for any occasion" — Provided by publisher.
  Audience: Grades 4 to 6.
  Includes bibliographical references and index.
  ISBN 978-1-63362-369-9 (lib. bdg.) — ISBN 978-1-63362-397-2
(pbk.) — ISBN 978-1-63362-425-2 (pdf) — ISBN 978-1-63362-453-5
(e-book)
  1. Party decorations—Juvenile literature. 2. Handicraft—Juvenile
literature. I. Title. II. Series: How-to library.

  TT900.P3R38 2016
  745.594'1—dc23   2014045643

Cherry Lake Publishing would like to acknowledge the work of The
Partnership for 21st Century Skills. Please visit www.p21.org for more
information.

Printed in the United States of America
Corporate Graphics
July 2015

A NOTE TO ADULTS:
Please review the instructions for these craft projects before your children make them. Be sure to help them with any steps you do not think they can safely do on their own.

A NOTE TO KIDS:
Be sure to ask an adult for help with these craft activities when you need it. Always put your safety first!

TABLE OF CONTENTS

Gifts for Your Guests

What kind of party do you want to throw?

Parties are a fun way to celebrate an occasion with friends. Birthdays, holidays, good-byes, welcome-homes, sporting events, and exciting accomplishments are all good reasons to throw a big bash.

As the party host, you have a lot to do! You need to plan the party's theme. You need to make a guest list and send out invitations. You also need to hang decorations, set the table, and provide lots of tasty food to eat. Whew!

Your job isn't done when the party starts, either. You need to greet everyone when they arrive. You need to make sure that your plans run smoothly and your guests have a good time. But you also need to make sure you are having a good time, too, even if you're busy!

You can keep the fun going long after the party ends by passing out party favors. A party favor is a gift from you to your guests. Goody bags are popular favors. These bags are often filled with candy, toys, pencils, or other fun treats. But you can also give out handmade party favors that are extra special and memorable—because you made them yourself!

Goody bags don't need to be shaped like bags!

Sticking to a Budget

Figuring out a budget will help you avoid spending too much money on your party.

The cost of throwing a party can add up. You need food, decorations, games, and, of course, favors! Make a **budget** to help you decide how much money you can spend on favors.

The cost for each party favor will depend on how many guests you plan to invite. If you are only inviting two or three friends, you may be able to spend more on party favors than if you have 15 or 20 guests.

Let's do the math. If have a budget of $25 and you have 5 guests, then you can spend $5 on each party favor. But if your budget is $25 and you have 20 guests, that's only $1.25 per party favor. You might want to rethink your budget and guest list. Or you can think of creative ways to save money!

Ways to Save

- Make things instead of buying them! The more you make yourself, the more money you'll save.
- Use recycled materials. Check your home for craft supplies or other materials that you can turn into something new.
- Have your party favors do double duty! Party favors can also serve as the centerpiece for your party table (see Sweet Wands on page 20), place cards for each seat (see Treat Boxes on page 13), decorations for hanging (see Treasure Ornaments on page 16), or activities at the party (see Sleepover Shams on page 28).

Your party might be more fun if you invite many guests, but it will also be more expensive!

Basic Tools

You'll need all sorts of craft materials to make party favors. Before you head out to the store, check at home for supplies you may already have.

You will need drawing, measuring, and cutting tools. These include pencils, rulers, markers, scissors, and hole punches. Paint pens can draw on surfaces other than paper. Fabric markers are for fabric!

Adhesives such as white glue, clear tape, and double-stick tape will help hold your projects together. Binder clips help hold fabric tight.

You will also need various types of paper. Cardboard is good for when you need stiff support for your project. Cardstock is a thick paper that comes in various colors, **textures**, and designs. White copy paper is good for sketching and other projects. Scraps of any type of paper—even wrapping paper and magazine pages—are useful for some projects.

There's no end to the items you can use for decoration! Here are just a few examples:

- Ribbon, string, jute, and lace
- Feathers
- Cotton balls
- Sequins and beads
- Glitter
- Stickers
- Confetti and streamers

You will probably need to go to the store for some supplies, such as:

- Candy, sprinkling sugar, and lollipop sticks
- Small and large clear treat bags
- Cupcake liners
- Pin backings
- Glass plates
- Washcloths and manicure supplies
- Plastic ornaments
- Pillowcases

For some of the projects in this book, you will need to use an oven and an iron. Always ask an adult for help with these appliances. Both can burn you, so you must be careful and pay attention.

Painting Tips

You need more than paint and a paintbrush. Use a paper plate as a **palette** to hold and mix your paint. Keep a container of water handy to clean your brush between colors. Use a paper towel to **blot** water and paint from your brush.

Thinking Outside the Bag

Goody bags can be filled with fun reminders of your party. But the outsides of the bags don't have to be boring. Decorate your bags with bling!

You can buy colorful bags at gift or craft stores. But check at home first. Do you collect gift bags from presents you've received? Do you keep small bags from shopping trips? You can jazz up these bags to hold goodies, too.

Fancy Bag

Raid your sewing basket for scraps of lace or ribbon to use as decoration. Use a hole punch to make holes around the top of the bag. Weave the ribbon in and out of the holes, and tie the loose ends in a bow. Glue a strip of lace along the bottom of the bag.

Winter Wonderland Bag

Glue cotton balls all around the top edge of the bag. Glue dots of white confetti on the rest of the bag to look like falling snow.

Feather Fun Bag

Glue a row of feathers around the top of the bag to make trim. Then glue on a strip of ribbon to hide the rough edges of the feathers.

Nature Bag

Collect natural treasures such as flowers and leaves. Tie them into a little bundle with a piece of jute. Use glue to attach the bundle to the front of the bag.

Creative Containers

Think of other creative containers you can make or use for your guests' goodies. For a western party, tuck the goodies into a bandana and tie it up with a piece of leather. If you are having a beach party, put the goodies in a small plastic pail. For a pizza party, ask your local pizza restaurant if you can have a few extra boxes for your friends!

Craft stores sell jars, mini paint cans, and take-out boxes to hold treats. You can also put treats in water bottles, mugs, and ceramic pots. Paint pens and permanent markers are useful to write your guests' names on these types of containers.

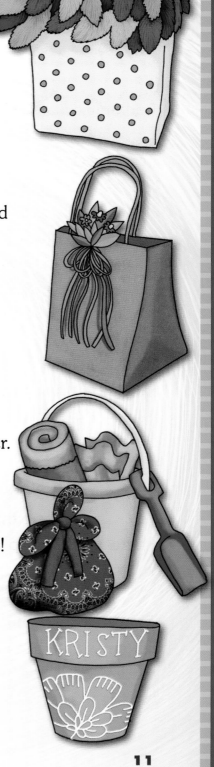

Whose Bag Is Whose?

Add an extra creative touch to any bag or container with homemade name tags. First, think about your theme. Use your imagination! It's fun to transform colored paper and other materials into tags for your friends.

Mermaid party

Blue paper can be a base for a green glitter name. Decorate it with pink shell stickers.

Robot party

Use glossy silver and red paper. Glue on bolts and other small pieces of hardware.

Summer party

Use yellow and orange paper, like the sunshine!

Pizza party

Use scraps of yellow, red, and green paper to put pizza toppings on a triangle-shaped tag.

Punch a hole in the corner of your tag, and then thread a piece of ribbon or string through it. This will let you wear the tag around your neck or attach it to a goody bag.

Treat Boxes

At formal occasions, such as weddings, there are often boxes of chocolates, almonds, or other sweet treats awaiting guests at their spots at the table. These treat boxes can work double duty as place cards. Write a guest's name on each box. Then place the boxes where you want your friends to sit.

Materials

- 12-inch by 12-inch (30.5 centimeter by 30.5 centimeter) cardstock
- Other scraps of paper for decoration
- Ruler
- Pencil
- Scissors
- Markers
- White glue or double-stick tape

Steps

1. Draw a 3-inch (7.6 cm) square in the middle of the cardstock. Continue the lines out to the edges of the paper. You'll have a cross shape with arms 3 inches (7.6 cm) wide.

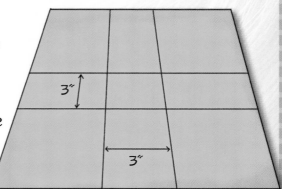

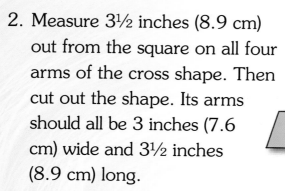

2. Measure 3½ inches (8.9 cm) out from the square on all four arms of the cross shape. Then cut out the shape. Its arms should all be 3 inches (7.6 cm) wide and 3½ inches (8.9 cm) long.

3. On the top arm, measure and mark 1½ inches (3.8 cm) in from the edge. Cut in on the line from the left. Only cut halfway to the middle point. Repeat on the bottom arm, but cut to the middle from the right this time. These slots will fit into each other to hold your box together.

4. On the side arms, draw triangles from the corner points to the middle of each edge. Cut along these lines.

5. Lift the two side triangles to the center and overlap them.

6. Next, bring the top and bottom arms to the center and over the triangles. Slip one slot into the other. Now you have a basic box.

7. To decorate your box for a specific theme, cut out a 3-inch (7.6 cm) square from another piece of paper. Fold it in half and cut out a **symmetrical** shape, such as a butterfly, heart, flower, or baseball.

8. Use markers and pens to add details to your shape. Then cut the shape in half along the fold line.

9. Unfold your box and turn it over so the bottom faces up. With glue or double-stick tape, attach half of your image to each end of the rectangular flaps. Be careful not to overlap the slot lines.

10. Flip the box back over. Place a few pieces of candy in the middle. Then fold your box back up as in steps 5 and 6.

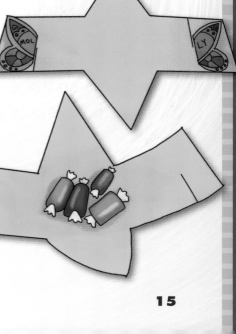

TIP!
This basic pattern can be adapted for any party theme. Also, you only need to measure once. Make a **template** that you can use over again to make more boxes.

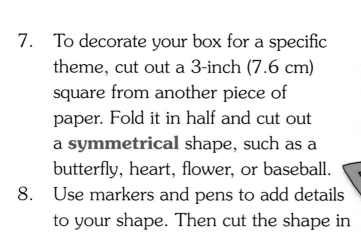

Treasure Ornaments

Ornaments are fun decorations for any party. They're even better when they're filled with candy and treasures! Finding these treasure-filled treats can be a party activity. Hang the ornaments in hidden places around your yard or in your home. Then set your friends loose to discover their treasure treats!

Materials

- Plastic ornaments
- Small candies
- Plastic rings
- Tinsel, streamers, or confetti
- 12-inch (30.5 cm) lengths of ribbon or string

Steps

1. Fill up the ornament with candy, rings, tinsel, and any other small treasures you can fit inside.

2. Click the two sides of the ornament closed.

3. Thread the ribbon through the holes on top of the ornament. Secure it with a knot.

4. Decide where you are going to hang your ornaments and think up some clues. If you hang your ornament on a swing set, the clue could be "Your treasure is in the place where we play." If you hide it in a closet, the clue could be "Your treasure is hanging out with some clothes!"

Personalized Painted Plates

Every guest will feel right at home with a plate **monogrammed** with his or her initial.

Materials

- Clear glass dinner plate
- Scissors
- Paper and pencil
- Clear tape
- Various colors of enamel acrylic paint (made for painting on glass)
- Paintbrushes, paper plate, paper towel, and water (see Painting Tips on page 9)
- Oven

Steps

1. Place the glass plate on the paper and draw a circle around the bottom. Cut out the circle. Draw your design—but draw it as a mirror image of the way you want it to appear on the plate. This is especially important when drawing letters!
2. Clean the glass plate well with warm water and dish soap. Dry it thoroughly. Then tape your design facedown on top of the

plate in the center. Flip the plate over. You will be painting on the bottom of the plate.

3. Squeeze out a little paint onto your palette. Use your brush to paint the areas of one color first. Let it dry a little before you add more colors. Try not to overlap your colors. (From the other side, you will only be able to see the areas you paint directly onto the plate.)

4. Next, you need to **cure** the paint so it will not wash off. First, check the directions on the paint bottle in case there are specific instructions for curing that brand. If there are no special instructions, put your plate into an oven, painted side up. Close the door, then set the oven to 350 degrees Fahrenheit (177 degrees Celsius). Heat the plate for 30 minutes. Then turn off the oven, but keep the door closed. Let the oven and plate cool down together (this may take a few hours).

REMINDER!
Ask an adult to help you use the oven.

After curing, the plate can be used for eating and can be hand-washed without washing away the paint. Remember not to paint your design on the top of the plate! It is not safe to eat food that comes in direct contact with the paint, even if the paint has been cured.

Sweet Wands

If your group of guests is the glittery type, create a display of shiny lollipops to use as a decorative centerpiece on your party table. When the party is over, take apart the display and give each guest a sparkly wand to bring some of the magic home!

Materials

- Oven
- Baking sheet
- Parchment paper
- Round hard candies in various colors
- Oven mitt
- Sprinkling sugar
- Long lollipop sticks
- Small clear candy bags
- One 24-inch (61 cm) lengths of 1/8-inch (0.3 cm) ribbon (per lollipop)
- Sequins and beads

REMINDER!
Ask an adult to help you use the oven.

Steps

1. Preheat the oven to 300°F. Line the baking sheet with parchment paper. Unwrap three candies. Place two on one end

of the baking sheet and one on the other. You will only be making three lollipops at a time. This will leave enough room for the candies to spread out and to add the sticks.

2. Bake the candies for 5 to 6 minutes, until they have completely melted. Remove the baking sheet from the oven with the oven mitt and immediately sprinkle the hot candies with sprinkling sugar.

3. Working quickly, place a stick into the center of each lollipop and turn it over immediately so that both sides of the stick are coated with melted candy. Let the candy cool completely (about 30 minutes). Repeat steps 1 to 3 to make more lollipops if needed.

4. Place a small candy bag over each lollipop.

5. String sequins and beads onto the ribbon. Tie it into a bow at the base of the lollipop.

HOW TO DISPLAY

Place a piece of Styrofoam or floral foam into a vase or pot. Stick the lollipops into the foam. Fill in the extra space in the vase or pot with colorful tissue paper.

Washcloth Candies

If you're planning a spa party, this favor will help guests pamper themselves later, too. Wrap up everything needed for a manicure in a neat little package that looks like candy! Display the washcloth candies in a bowl for guests to grab on their way out of the party.

Materials

- Large clear treat bag
- Scissors
- Colorful washcloth
- Nail polish, nail file, and hand lotion
- Clear tape
- Two pieces of ribbon, cut into 12-inch (30.5 cm) lengths

Steps

1. Cut the end off the treat bag so you have a plastic sleeve that is open on both ends. Set it aside.
2. Fold the washcloth in half. Place the nail polish, nail file, and hand lotion on one end.

3. Roll them up inside the washcloth from bottom to top as snugly as you can.
4. Slip the washcloth into the plastic sleeve. Then roll the sleeve tightly around the cloth and tape it closed.
5. Gather one end of the sleeve and tie it with a piece of ribbon in a tight bow. Repeat on the other side.

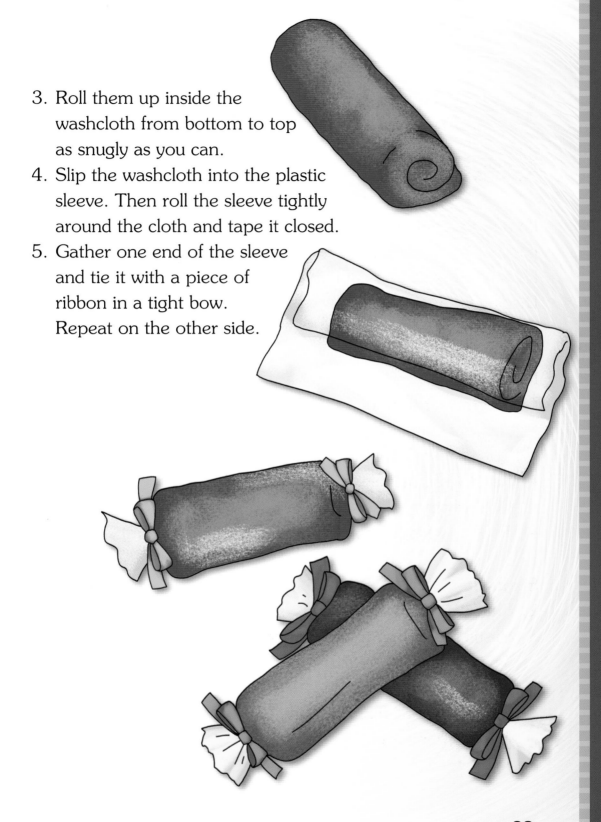

Celebrity Autograph Books

This party favor does double duty as a fun activity. Pass out these autograph books to your friends. Then have them sit in a circle. Ask them to hand their books to the people to their right to sign. Keep passing the books along so that everyone has a turn to sign everyone else's book. Your guests will go home with a book full of autographs and some extra pages for their own celebrity sightings!

Materials

- Glittery cardstock paper, cut into two 5½-by-8½-inch (14 by 21.6 cm) rectangles
- Ruler
- Scissors
- Hole punch
- 20 pieces of white copy paper, cut in half (5½ by 8½ inches, or 14 by 21.6 cm)
- One 24-inch (61 cm) length of ribbon, plus some extra
- Stickers
- Markers
- Pen or pencil

Steps

1. On one of the pieces of cardstock, measure 1 inch (2.5 cm) from the shorter edge on the non-glittery side. Use the edge of the scissors to **score** a line. This will be your front cover.
2. On this same edge, measure 1½ inches (3.8 cm) down from the top and 1½ inches (3.8 cm) up from the bottom. Make marks with a pencil. Punch a hole at each mark.
3. Use these holes as a template to mark the other piece of cardstock, which will be the back cover. Punch the holes. Then use the template to mark the white copy paper, about 5 at a time. Punch the holes in these as well.
4. Place the sheets on your work surface in this order: the back cover (undecorated side up), then the 40 inside pages, and then the front cover (decorated side up). Line up all of the holes.
5. Thread the ends of the 24-inch (61 cm) length of ribbon up through the holes. Pull the ribbon tight so it lays flat on the back of the book. Tie a bow on the front. Use stickers or markers to add the name of a guest to the front of the book.
6. Tie small lengths of ribbon around the end of a pencil or pen.

Award Ribbons

Games and contests can be exciting entertainment at a party. For these types of activities, you'll need prizes for the winners! Make your own award ribbon pins to celebrate a job well done.

Materials

- Paper cupcake liners
- Scissors
- Ruler
- Scraps of cardstock paper in various colors
- White glue
- Four pieces of ¼-inch (0.6 cm) ribbon cut into 5-inch (12.7 cm) lengths for each award
- Cardboard
- Pin backing

Steps

1. Fold a cupcake liner in half. Cut off about ½ inch (1.3 cm) from around the edge. Then cut small slits from the edge to the center circle all around. The liner can now lie flat.

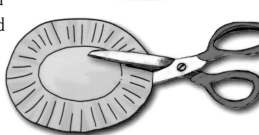

2. Cut out a cardstock circle that is the same size as the center circle of the paper liner. Then cut out other shapes to decorate your award, such as stars, flowers, or smaller circles.

3. Glue the cardstock circle to the center of the liner. Then glue the other paper decorations on top of the circle.

4. Flip the liner over. Glue the ends of the four ribbon pieces onto the back of the liner so they stick out diagonally from the center.

5. Cut out a disc of cardboard that is the same size as the back circle of the cupcake liner. Glue it over the ends of the ribbons, pressing down well.

6. Glue a pin backing onto the cardboard disc. Let the glue dry completely before wearing the award!

Sleepover Shams

Plan this super-easy activity to help fill up the time at a sleepover party. Decorating pillowcases fits the theme perfectly. Your guests will remember your party every time they go to sleep!

Materials

- White or light-colored pillowcase
- Large piece of cardboard, about the same size as the pillowcase
- Eight binder clips
- Fabric markers
- Iron

Steps

1. Slip the cardboard into the pillowcase.
   Pull the fabric tightly all around and secure it with binder clips.
2. Use fabric markers to draw pictures on your pillowcase.
   You can write names or fun sayings and jokes, too.
3. Remove the clips and the cardboard. Ask an adult to iron the back of the pillowcase. This sets the marker ink so it won't wash off in the washing machine. Directions may vary for different fabric markers, so be sure to check the instructions for your specific brand.

Never-Ending Party

The fun doesn't have to end just because your party is over. A party favor is a way for guests to bring a little bit of the fun home. It's like a never-ending party!

Party favors can be so much more than just a bag of candy.
- They can be the decorations and activities for your party.
- They are thank-you gifts to your friends.
- They show off your unique creative talents.
- They are a fun reminder of a celebration.
- Most of all, they show your guests that you care enough to take the time to make something special for them.

You're special, too. (And not just because you throw a good party!) Remember to make a party favor for yourself!

Your friends will never forget your party!

Glossary

adhesives (ad-HEE-sivz) substances used to stick two objects together

blot (BLAHT) to dry by pressing lightly

budget (BUH-jit) a plan for how to spend money

cure (KYUR) to preserve or harden something, often through drying

monogrammed (MAH-noh-gramd) having a design made from letters, usually someone's initials

palette (PA-lit) a flat surface for holding or mixing paint

score (SKOR) to make indented lines in paper or some other material

symmetrical (si-MEH-trik-uhl) exactly the same on both sides of a center line

template (TEM-plit) a pattern used to make the same shape multiple times

textures (TEKS-churz) the different ways things feel

For More Information

Books

Andrus, Aubre. *Slumber Wonders: Make All Your Slumber Party Dreams Come True*. Middleton, WI: American Girl Publishing, 2012.

Daulter, Anni, et al. *Naturally Fun Parties for Kids: Creating Handmade, Earth-Friendly Celebrations for All Seasons and Occasions*. South Portland, ME: Sellers Pub., 2012.

Kenney, Karen L. *Cool Theme Parties: Perfect Party Planning for Kids*. Minneapolis: ABDO, 2012.

Lyden, Kelly. *Stylish Kids' Parties: Recipes & Decorations for 12 Festive Occasions*. Blue Ash, OH: KP Craft, 2014.

Rau, Dana Meachen. *Dessert Designer: Creations You Can Make and Eat!* North Mankato, MN: Capstone Young Readers, 2013.

Web Sites

Better Homes and Gardens: Fun Birthday Party Favors for Kids
www.bhg.com/party/birthday/party-games/fun-birthday-party-favors-for-kids/
This page is filled with ideas for easy-to-make favors for your guests.

Family Education: Parties and Gifts
http://fun.familyeducation.com/parties/entertainment/39547.html
Find ideas for fun ways to throw a party.

PBS Parents: Birthday Party Etiquette
www.pbs.org/parents/birthday-parties/tips_post/birthday-party-etiquette/
Pick up tips that will help you be a good host.

Index

About the Author

Dana Meachen Rau is the author of more than 300 books for children on many topics, including science, history, cooking, and crafts. She creates, experiments, researches, and writes from her home office in Burlington, Connecticut.